see this

jane yolen

little

laëtitia devernay

dot

creative
editions

See this little dot?
It's not
just a blot
on a page.

Not just a spot
of ink
on a shirt.

Or a bit of dirt
on the back
of your shoe.

It's not just the wide-open eye

of a cat

or a dog

or a crow
or a bat.

Not a marble,
or a ball,
or an unfilled space.

See, this little dot,
it's got
no squiggle.

It does not wiggle
like a worm on a hook.

This dot can be as big
as the moon in the sky.
It can be as tiny as
the eye on a fly.

It usually waits,
content with its job.
Small, complete,
very neat.
Not messy
like a blob.

It's perfect
and it's round.
It has oomph, roll, and zest.

Sometimes it bounces
HIGH.
Or falls real
LOW.

It mostly stays at rest.

So, see this little dot?
It's my very good friend.
And what it does best
is at

The
End.

Library of Congress Cataloging-in-Publication Data

Names: Yolen, Jane, author. / Devernay, Laëtitia, 1982- , illustrator.

Title: See this little dot / by Jane Yolen; illustrated by Laëtitia

Devernay. Description: Mankato, MN: Creative Editions, 2024. /

Audience: Ages 5–7. / Audience: Grades K–1. / Summary:

Illustrates the characteristics and possible functions of a dot.

Identifiers: LCCN 2023013383 (print) / LCCN 2023013384

(ebook) / ISBN 9781568463827 (hardcover) /

ISBN 9781640006768 (pdf)

Subjects: CYAC: Dot (Symbol)—Fiction. / LCGFT: Picture books.

Classification: LCC PZ7.Y78 Sbh 2024 (print) /

LCC PZ7.Y78 (ebook) / DDC [E]—dc23

LC record available at https://lccn.loc.gov/2023013383

LC ebook record available at https://lccn.loc.gov/2023013384

9 8 7 6 5 4 3 2